PICTURES OF
PRAGUE

KAROL BENICKÝ

PICTURES OF
PRAGUE

ENGLISH VERSION

Author: Karol Benický
Text: Jiří Karbaš
Grafic design: Karol Benický, Denisa Jobová
Translation: Carla Tkadlečková, Iva Švajcrová
104 pages, 168 photos
Print preparation: Milan JOB-DTP studio, Příbram
Printed by PBtisk, s. r. o., Příbram, 2006

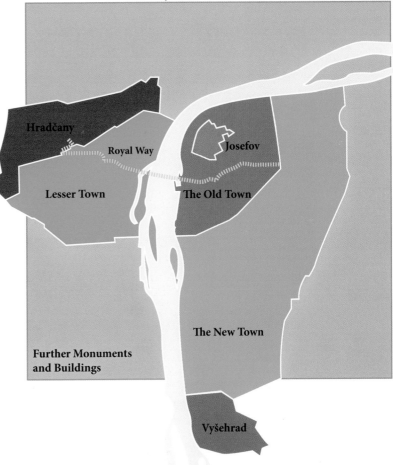

Hradčany

Royal Way

Josefov

Lesser Town

The Old Town

The New Town

Further Monuments
and Buildings

Vyšehrad

INTRODUCTION

"I vision a town so great that its fame and glory will reach the stars", says the mythic princess Libuše in her prophecy, as it is described by Alois Jirásek in the Old Czech Legends, when she challenges her court to build a castle and call it Prague as the place where to find Man carving the threshold (in Czech prah) of his house.

No other town in the world can come up to Prague in variety and richness of architectonical monuments and its location in a green scenery like the hills Prague is surrounded by, with the River Vltava flowing through the town a wavy ribbon like. Down to the present days, churches of pre-Romanesque and Romanesque style as well as a wide range of Romanesque houses and palaces have survived. The Gothic left not only St. Vitus's Cathedral which has been the symbol of the Czech statehood for centuries, and the picturesque silhouette of the Prague castle. Impressive buildings of ecclesiastical and domestic architecture date back to those days as well. The Italian Renaissance left its marks in Prague in the form of splendid summer-houses and palaces surrounded by flowery gardens with wonderful statues. Baroque, probably the last universal architectural style in Europe whose artistic and creative aspects interfere even in modern architecture, made Prague a metropolis of European importance whose ecclesiastical and secular buildings made it comparable to Rome in its importance. Plentiful are the marks of Rococo and Classicism, multifaceted and rich the historistic architectonical styles of the 19th century and Czech Cubism, a style which was given birth to in Prague and underwent its first development there.

Prague is fabulously rich in archaeological monuments that prove the development of the Czech state from the very beginnings of the rise of the historical town of Prague. The monuments in other districts than the very heart of Prague, which, in their origin, were villages in the neighbourhood of the town and, step by step, affiliated to the historical centre during the 19th and in the beginning of the 20th century becoming its integral parts, are of significant importance as well.

In the course of its more than thousands years of development, Prague has become a town of architects, painters, musicians, poets, and other artists who gradually formed its image in the eyes of Europe. It has been one of the most important European cities ever since, hosting kings and emperors, being visited by popes, offering a place where to live and work for artists as Mozart, the 250th anniversary of whose birthday celebrates the whole world of culture this year.

Waldstein's Garden – Lesser Town

PRAGUE CASTLE – HRADČANY

From the historical point of view, the Prague Castle was established in the end of the 9th century by a prince of the famous line of the Přemyslids as a mansion house and county seat of the Czechs lands. At the same time, it was founded to protect the market village on the banks of the River Vltava from which Prague arose. Being originally a wooden Slavonic fortification including three churches made of stone which were gradually built between 890 and 935 (the Church of Our Lady, St. George's Basilica, and the original s. Vitus Cathedral), in the 11th and 12th century, the castle developed into a Romanesque place with stone fortifications, the royal palace, two basilicas, a Benedictine monastery, houses of the bishop, and chapter houses. During the reign of Přemysl Otakar II., new fortifications and the Gothic palace were built; the later was subject to further construction under Charles IV. (after 1336). In the middle of the 14th century, the construction of the choir of the new St. Vitus Cathedral with the big spire was set about by Peter Parléř and his guild. After 1486, during the reign of the Polish dynasty of the Jagellonians, the great hall in the Palace called Wladislaw Hall after the king Wladislaw Jagello was built. This hall was the biggest one in the medieval Prague. Today it is used on the occasion of the election of the president of the Czech Republic, important celebrations of national importance are held here. The architect Benedict Ried of Pístov is the author of the challenging vault of the hall with its groined stars, the windows were conceived Renaissance like.

Under Ferdinand I., the Italian garden was created with the Renaissance summer-house called Queen Anna's Palace and the ball house. After 1584, under the emperor Rudolf II., the new palaces in the northern and southern part of the complex including the Spanish Hall and the Gallery were built. In the middle of the 18th century, during the reign of Maria Theresia, all buildings except the Old Royal Palace underwent a Baroque alteration after a project by Nicola Pacassi. The first court of the castle also dates back to this project. In the years 1873–1929, St. Vitus Cathedral was accomplished by the architects Josef Mocker and Kamil Hilbert. The New Palace was altered in accordance with the project by Josip Plečnik, and in 1918, Prague Castle became the seat of the Head of the Czech Government and nowadays of the Czech state.

Hradčany, chronologically from the point of view of its development the third historical district of Prague, was founded by the governor of the castle Berka of Dubé around 1320. Originally, it was only a square. In the course of the centuries, three parts of this town developed. After 1541, Renaissance palaces of the courtiers as well as churches were built in the neighbourhood of the square. In Pohořelec, the bourgeoisie settled, and in the New World, the poor got their homes. In the 17th century, further palaces as Thun, Sternberg, Martinic and the Archiepiscopal Palace were built, furthermore, Czernin Palace and, in 1694, Loreta with its famous glockenspiel by the clock maker Peter Naumann. In 1726, a statue of Our Lady by Ferdinand Maxmilian Brokof was established in the centre of the square. As the result of the castle alteration by Pacassi, the moat between the castle itself and the settlement nearby was removed providing then direct access to the castle from the square and connecting the castle with the quarter of Hradčany.

The Lesser Town Tower of Charles Bridge, St. Nicholas Church and Prague castle

Hradčany Square, left – Schwarzenberg Palace, Toscana Palace in the background

Main Aisle of St. Vitus Cathedral

St. George's equestrian statue in the third courtyard

Gravestone of Saint John of Nepomuk

The Chapel of All Saints – Prague castle

Archbishop Palace in Hradčany Square

Old Parliament House of the Prague Castle

Main Aisle of the Basilica of St. George

Loreto of Prague in Hradčany – the Church of the Birth of Our Lord

Lesser Town, view from Hradčany

The New World in Hradčany

The Old Castle steps of the Prague Castle

Prague Castle. Seat of the President

Ledebur Garden

Loreto of Prague in Loreto Square

The gothic Wladislaw Hall of Prague Castle

The Castle Guard

Saint John of Nepomuk Chapel

Daliborka Tower

Holy Cross Chapel in Prague Castle

Hradčany and Lesser Town Skyline

Saint Rochus Church (MIRO Galery) – Strahov courtyard

The Prague Castle – sculpture on the Main Gate

The Prague Castle – sculpture on the Main Gate

Golden Gate – St. Vitus Cathedral

Sternberk Palace – National Gallery

St. Vitus Cathedral – view with gargoyles

Gothic vault – The Old Royal Palace

Gothic vault above the Hunting Stairs

View of Lesser Town from St. Vitus Cathedral

Chotek Gardens in Hradčany

Belvedere of Queen Ann in the Prague Castle

St. Vitus Cathedral. St. Wenceslas Chapel

Pastophorium of St. Wenceslas Chapel

Rose window of St. Vitus Cathedral

Stain-glass pane by Alfons Mucha in St. Vitus Cathedral

Stain-glass panes above the altar in St. Vitus Cathedral

Basilica of St. George at Christmas time

Strahov Monastery, the seat of the Premonstratensian Order

The Prague Castle from Petřín

Czernin Palace – Ministry of Foreign Affairs

St. Vitus Cathedral – Baroque organ

The Chamber of Provincial Plates in the Old Royal Palace

Golden Lane in the Prague Castle

Theological Hall of the Strahov Library

The Big Library Hall of the Strahov Monastery

LESSER TOWN

In the year 1257, king Přemysl Otakar II. established the second town of Prague in a location where a market settlement had existed from the 9th century. The centre of that town was its today's square with St. Nicolas's which dates back to 1283. From the square, roads led towards the bridge, furthermore to the castle, to Újezd and the monastery of St. Thomas's. An important architecture of international value was the Johannites monastery which was established in the middle of the 12th century, and the residence of the bishop. Under Charles IV., in the second half of the 14th century, the town exceeded till Újezd. Those days, the so called Greedy Wall was built which leads through the hillside of Petrin to the hilltop. In 1419, the Lesser Town burnt down to the ground. Fire also spread out in 1503 and 1541. After them and after the Battle on the White Mountain in the beginning of the 17th century, the construction of spacious palaces of the aristocracy and the clergy began. Waldstein Palace with its wonderful garden and the statues of Antique Gods by Adrian de Vries arose as well as Lichtenstein Palace, Michnov Palace, Slavata Palace, and others. A number of old medieval houses and narrow streets fell victim for those ostentatious buildings. In the course of the 18th century, new Baroque palaces with gardens rich in fountains, statues and flower beds as Ledeburg garden, Vrtba garden, Kolowrat garden, etc. were being built. They boarder the shoulder of the castle hill giving the romantic maze of narrow streets and lanes between them, which still invite for a stroll in the summer evenings full of sweet smells of the flowers and the twitter of the birds in the gardens, their final image. In many a garden, theatre is played or concerts of classical music esp. Baroque music are held.

Today, the Lesser Town is above all a picture of Baroque architecture and architecture of the 19th century, a poetic maze of streets which lead from the Castle through Neruda Street and Mostecka Street to Charles Bridge or through Karmelitska Street up the hill of Petrin. In Karmelitska Street, in the Church of Our Lady Victorious there is the famous statue of the Infant Jesus, a Spanish work made from wax dating back to the 16th century. The statue was devoted the church by Polyxena of Lobkovice in 1628. St. Nicolas's in Lesser Town Square still remains the very heart of the Lesser Town as it used to be in former times. The only difference is its fascinating and monumental Baroque style which is the result of the alteration carried out by Christoph and Kilian Ignaz Dienzenhofer, architects of European importance, between 1704 and 1755.

The whole Lesser Town retained its original old-timey and crinoline beauty and mainly its historical genuineness. Hardly anywhere else in Europe with the exception of Italy, such an admirable complex of history, grace and charm can be found in many a gable or house sign as At the Two suns, At the Three Violins, At the Golden Cup, etc. in Neruda Street and others. The view on the roofs of the Lesser Town that opens from the Prague Castle is one of the most unforgettable experiences one can have; it is a view into a different time and different ages.

St. Nicholas Church

Waldstein Garden with a view of Hradčany

Charles Bridge and Lesser Town

View of Petřín from the Lesser Town embankment

Lesser Town Kampa in winter

The Isle of Kampa in winter

View of the Houses of Parliament in Lesser Town Square

The famous Bambino of Prague in the Church of Our Lady

The Church of St. Laurence on Petřín hill

Vrtba Garden – Lesser Town

Lesser Town in Winter

Lesser Town roofs

Herget's Brick Factory – Museum of Franz Kafka

The baroque dome of St. Nicholas in Lesser Town Square

Neruda Street – Lesser Town

Waldstein Palace – the main hall

A nook of the Isle of Kampa, Devil's brook (Čertovka)

Sala terrena in Waldstein's Garden – detail of the ceiling

"At the Three Small Violins" – House Sign

The Lesser Town

THE OLD TOWN

The Old Town of Prague was established in a place where originally a market settlement developed on the so called Jewish Flood Isle near the today's House of Artists where a crossing used to be, connecting the settlement with an old trade route from the east. As archaeological research has shown, in the neighbourhood of today's Široká Street there was probably the oldest market place. A further trade centre developed on the so called Slavonic Flood Isle, nevertheless the most important trade place was located in a place which now is known as Old Town Square with its Custom House at Ungelt. In the 12th and 13th centuries, there was a tensely populated settlement with residential tower houses made of stone. Some of them as e.g. the house At the Bell on the corner of Týnská Street and Old Town Square have survived and were notably refurbished. In the 30s of the 13th century, the so called Havel Town was established and in 1338, when the inhabitants of the Old Town were given the right to build a town hall, they built it in the today's Old Town Square which developed into the centre of the town. It was there where the new main Church of Our Lady before the Týn was located, a church in Gothic architecture with two high spires. In this church, the tombstone of Tychon de Brahe was laid in 1601, in the place where the famous Danish astronomer who worked on the court of Rudolf II. was buried.

Old Town Square has seen many an important event of Czech history, whether from the age of the Hussite movement or the execution of 27 Bohemian noblemen after the lost Battle on the White Mountain. Only two hundred metres from there, a different kind of history was written, a history of cultural and intellectual development. Near Old Town Square, Charles IV. established a university in 1348 which still works and is one of the oldest and most reputable universities in Europe. To get there follow Železná Street, and in its neighbourhood there is the Estates Theatre (originally Nostic Theatre) where in 1787 Mozart's Don Giovanni was premiered.

Further important architectonical monuments in the Old Town are e.g. the Monastery of St. Anna at František, the Bethlehem's Chapel and two Gothic spires which used to be the border to the town, the Old Town Bridge Tower at Charles Bridge, a work by Peter Parléř and his guild, and the Powder Tower whose architect was Matyáš Rejsek. Both the monuments underwent an alteration in the Neo-Renaissance style, nevertheless they kept their character as part of the fortification and their monumentality including wonderful statues. The Old Town as well as the Lesser Town takes pride in a range of Romanesque, Gothic, Renaissance, and Baroque architecture forming a unique historical unit of the styles.

The greatest jewel of Prague except the Prague Castle, Charles Bridge, is part of the Lesser Town as well as the Old Town. It was built in 1357 instead of the further Judith Bridge from the 12th century and accomplished in the beginning of the 15th century. Though the architect was Jan Ottl, the project and the construction itself was lead by Peter Parléř, the author of the Cathedral. The Baroque statues date back to the years 1683–1714. This is probably the most beautiful medieval bridge in Europe as its visitors claim.

The Old Town Square

Charles Bridge, the Old Town in the background

Charles Bridge – St. John of Nepomuk

Charles Bridge – Madonna with St. Bernard

Charles Bridge – Holy Cross sculpture (Calvary)

Charles Bridge – Statue of the Knight Bruncvík

Křižovnické Square with the statue of Charles IV., left – St. Francis of Assisi Church, St. Salvátor Church in the background

Clam-Gallas Palace – Heracles sculptures

Clam-Gallas Palace – Baroque staircase

"Golden Well House" (U Zlaté studny) in Karlova Street

Clam-Gallas Palace – Triton sculpture

51

At the Rotts' in Little Square in the Old Town

The Old Town Hall

The Old Town Hall – sculptures of the oriel chapel

"At the Minute" House (Dům U minuty)– renaissance facade

Clementinum – Baroque Hall of the Knights of the Cross

54   *The Old Town Square. Rococo Golz-Kinsky Palace, The Church of Our Lady of Týn and "At the White Unicorn" House*

Musicians in the Old Town Square, St. Nicholas Church in the background

The Astronomical Clock in Old Town Square

Art Nouveau facade of the Municipal House

The Municipal House – ceiling by Alfons Mucha

The Lord Mayor cabinet of the Minicipal House

Decoration of the main entrance of the Municipal House

Tourist Paradise at the Charles Bridge

Ungelt – Granovsky Palace

The Spires of Prague. Novotný Bridge

Drink water fountain in Příkopy

Na Příkopě – one of Prague's pedestrian precincts

The Municipal Hall – an Art Nouveau element

Paris Hotel - a mosaic detail above the entrance

The Municipal Hall – Art Nouveau decoration of the porch

Ungelt – a corner bear statue

The Municipal House with the Powder Tower

The Entrance area of St. Agnes Monastery

Estates Theatre (Stavovské divadlo) in Železná Street

Bethlehem Chapel in Bethlehem Square

The church of St. Aegidius

les University

Baroque bay of St. Jacob Basilica – Malá Štupartská

Clementinum – the baroque library hall

Rudolphinum – concert and exhibition halls

St. Francis of Assisi Church , Křižovnické Square – a detail from the main altar

Estates Theatre and the oriel window of the Carolinum Chapel

Coal Market –a fountain with F. X. Lederer sculpture

THE JEWISH TOWN (JOSEFOV)

The Jewish Town developed in the Early Middle Ages together with the Old Town being part of it, nevertheless it was separated from it by walls and gates and kept so its autonomy and self administration. Life in the Jewish Town was concentrated around several synagogues among which the so called Old New Synagogue from the second half of the 13th century is the oldest and, from the architectonical point of view, also the most beautiful one. It was built in Early Gothic style in today's Paris Street. In its neighbourhood, there is the Old Jewish Cemetery which was established in the first half of the 15th century and served for its purpose till 1768. There are approx. 12,000 tombs with the oldest one, the original Abigdora Kara, dating back to 1439. On this cemetery, there is the Renaissance tombstone of the famous rabbi Jehuda Liw ben Becalel (the so called rabbi Löw who died in 1609 and is connected with the widely known Prague legend of the Golem). Furthermore, in the Old Jewish Cemetery there were buried prominent people as the primate of the Jewish Town Mordechaj Maisel (who died in 1601) and the rabbi and collector of Hebraic manuscript books David Oppenheim (died in 1736).

Between 1590 and 1592, i.e. during the reign of Rudolf II., Maisel built a synagogue which got its name after him. The original Renaissance building underwent Baroque and Neo-Gothic alterations, today it serves for the purpose of an exhibition hall and the depositary of the Jewish Museum. Another synagogue, the Pinkas synagogue, was built in 1535 by Aron Meshullam Horovitz. Today, the collection of children's drawing from the concentration camp Theresienstadt from 1942–1944 is on display there. The Klaus Synagogue is situated in the very neighbourhood of the Old Jewish Cemetery. The building of the synagogue rose after a fire had broken out in the ghetto in 1689, and was accomplished in 1694. In the 80s of the 19th century, it was reconstructed. Today it is home to the exhibition of Jewish traditions and customs. The latest synagogue is the Spanish one from 1868 which was built in Moorish architecture after a project by Vojtěch Ignaz Ullman. Today it hosts one part of the exhibition on the History of the Jewish people in Bohemia and Moravia, the other part of the exhibition is on display at the Maisel synagogue. All these synagogue as well as the Jewish Cemetery, the Town Hall, and the Ceremonial Hall, built by the architect J. Gerstl in pseudo Romanesque architecture between 1911–1912, are part of the complex of the Jewish Museum of Prague which was established in 1906 in the presence of the historian Dr Salomon Hugo Lieben and Dr Augustin Stein, the Chairman of the Jewish Community. The Old New Synagogue is except the High and Jerusalem Synagogues which do not belong to the Jewish Museum one of the three Prague Synagogues where services are held.

For centuries, the Jewish Town was not only the centre of trade and finance; it was as well a place where science at a high international level boomed. From the 16th century, this town was called ghetto being a labyrinth of narrow zigzagging streets being great only thanks to its patrician houses und the Town Hall. Under Josef II., the walls separating the Jewish Town from the Old Town were removed. Nevertheless it was only in 1848 when the town was included into Prague as one of its quarters called Josefov. After 1896, the larger part of this quarter was torn down because of the insufficient hygienic and living conditions there. The synagogues, the Town Hall, and the cemetery survived.

Not far from the complex of the Jewish Museum, there is the house of birth of the worldwide famous writer Franz Kafka in Franz Kafka Square between Maisel Street and Kaprova Street. Today there is a gallery. The Museum of Franz Kafka is situated at the so called Hergets' brick factory in Cihelná Street in the Lesser Town near the banks of the River Vltava.

The Old Jewish Cemetery – tombstone of Rabbi Löw

Hebrew clock on the Jewish Town Hall

Maisl Synagogue

Klaus Synagogue

Old Jewish Cemetery

The Old-New Synagogue

Tombstones at the Old Jewish Cemetery

Maisl Street with the building of the Jewish Town Hall

Old Jewish Cemetery

Pinkas Synagogue

Spanish Synagogue

THE NEW TOWN

The New Town was established by Charles IV. in 1348. Those days, it was an impressive urban work based on a carefully planned ground plan with three squares – Hay Square, Horse Square (today's Wenceslas Square), and Cattle Square (today's Charles Square). A network of streets was linked to them where mostly craftsmen and burghers lived. The dominant of the New Town under Charles IV. was the Church of Our Lady of the Snows with a Franciscan garden. This Cathedral, the tallest one in Prague, was established in 1347 by Charles IV. for the Carmelite Monastery in memory of the king's coronation. Nevertheless, the choir was built as the only part of the church which became the today's cathedral. Nevertheless one can imagine the gigantic building as it was originally planned. It would have been the greatest cathedral of Prague and one of the biggest in Europe.

The second dominant of the New Town was surely the New Town Hall with its corner tower which was built at the turn of the 14th and 15th century. Its today's appearance dates back to 1905 and is the result of an alteration by the architects Antonín Wiehle a Kamil Gilbert. The oldest building of the New Town is the Romanesque round church of St. Longinus in the Street Na Rybníčku dating back to the 12th century. The third monument of the Age of Charles IV. was the monastery church Na Slovanech which was built as a three-nave-church of Gothic architecture between 1347 and 1372. Today it is reconstructed, has a new façade developed by F. M. Černý in 1967.

The centre of the New Town and the whole Town of Prague is Wenceslas Square (formerly Horse Square) with the premises of the National Museum at its top, a building by Josef Schulz in Neo-Renaissance architecture, built between 1885 and 1890. In front of the National Museum, there is the Monument of St. Wenceslas, the patron of the Czech lands who was historically one of the first princes of the Přemyslids' line and died in 935. Author of the monument is the sculptor J. V. Myslbek. Around the monument, the statues of the Czech patrons St. Ludmila, Prokop, Anna, and Vojtěch are arranged. Another building of importance is the National Theatre on the banks of the River Vltava, which was created by Josef Schulz and Josef Zítek between 1868 and 1881 and built in the Neo-Renaissance style as well. A significant Art Nouveau building is the Municipal House in the Street Na Příkopě, an example of modern architecture is the Dancing House on Rašín Embankment.

The New Town Hall in the Charles Square

Wenceslas Square from the National Museum

Art Nouveau facade of the hotel 'Europe'

Franciscans Garden and Church of Mary of the Snows

St. Ignaz Church in the Charles Square

St. Constantin and Methodius Church – sculptures

The National Museum in the upper part of Wenceslas Square

Wenceslas Square – St. Wenceslas sculpture

Lock on the River Vltava

Emmaus Abbey (Monastery Na Slovanech)

Langhans House (centrum FotoŠkoda), Vodičkova Street

Euro Palace, Wenceslas Square

The Dancing House on the Rašín Embankment

National Theatre with Masaryk Embankment

Mánes Gallery on the Slavonic Isle

86

Side altar of St. Ignatius Church – Charles Square

National Museum – representative staircase

VYŠEHRAD

The Prince's Castle of Vyšehrad was established at one time or another in the 10th century on a rock high above the River Vltava. It was here where, according to the legend, the mythic princess Libuše foretold the glory and greatness of Prague. From the historical point of view, Vyšehrad was at the height of its power in the 11th century during the reign of Wladislaw II. of the line of the Přemyslids who built there a stone castle, established a chapter, three churches and improved the importance of Vyšehrad as the seat of the king. From this age, only the Romanesque round church of St. Martin's has survived which was built in the end of the 11th century. It is the oldest of the three round churches in Prague. The silhouette of the Rocks of Vyšehrad is accomplished by St. Peter and Paul's, a church which was built under Wladislaw II. Originally it was of Romanesque architecture, later under Charles IV. it was rebuilt in Gothic style, then in the 18th century baroquized, and in 1885–1887, when it got its today's image, rebuilt in Gothic architecture by Josef Mocker. Under Charles IV., Vyšehrad was only a 'second quality' dominant of the New Town of Prague. In the 17th century, a military citadel in Baroque style was built there and after its liquidation, the National Cemetery called Slavín (pantheon) was established instead of the local cemetery of Vyšehrad. Here the most important people of the Czech cultural life are buried. From the citadel, only the two Baroque gates, Tabor Gate and Leopold Gate, which date back to the second half of the 17th century survived. Tabor Gate was the first gate on the way to Prague from Pankrác, the only possible way to Vyšehrad when it became a military fortification. Leopold Gate which was built by Carlo Lurago, an Italian master builder and architect, is an example of north Italian fortress architecture of Early Baroque Classicism.

The church in Karlov nearby founded in 1350 by Charles IV. for the Augustine monastery is another monument of importance. It was accomplished in 1575 by Bonifaz Wolmut who provided it with the fabulous star vault of the cathedral's octagon. Its form is similar to the funeral church of Charles the Great in Aachen, the patron of Charles IV.

Impressive is the view that opens from Vyšehrad towards Zbraslav on the River Vltava underlining the importance of the strategic location, controlling the stream of the main Czech river and the gateway to Prague along the river.

Romanesque Rotunda of St. Martin

J. V. Myslbek – Slavoj and Záboj

J. V. Myslbek – Přemysl and Libuše

J. V. Myslbek – Ctirad and Šárka

J. V. Myslbek – Lumír and a Song

Leopold Gate

Portal of St. Peter and Paul's Church

Vyšehrad Cemetery arcade

Slavín in Vyšehrad Cemetery

St. Peter and Paul's Church with the River Vltava

Vyšehrad – St. Peter and Paul's Church

FURTHER MONUMENTS AND BUILDINGS (monuments and buildings in other districts of Prague)

Except the historical towns, a range of settlements, villages, and farmhouses dating back to the Early Middle Ages had existed on the territory of today's Prague. As they were extending they were gradually included into Prague as autonomic quarters of the town. The oldest quarter to the west of Prague is Břevnov where in 993 the first monks' monastery of the Czech lands was established. The most famous settlement of those that had been developing for centuries in the district of Smíchov, is probably Bertramka which was established in the 17th century and is famous for Wolfgang Amadeus Mozart's residence there from 1786 to 1789 who was host of the Dušek couple.

At the plain of the White Mountain, the deer-field Star together with the beautiful Renaissance summer house Star was established in 1530 as a project by Juan Aistalis and Giovanni Luchese who built the palace after 1555 for the archduke Ferdinand of Tyrol. The ground plan of the summer house is in form of a hexagram.

One of the important architectural monuments is, above all, the Exhibition Palace near the original deer park called familiarly Stromovka. This Palace was developed by the architect Bedřich Münzberger as the main building for the Jubilee Exhibition in Prague in 1891. Later, in 1907, it underwent an alteration on accordance to a project by Josef Fanta. For the purpose of that Exhibition in 1891, the cast-iron structure of the Hanavsky Pavilion was built which later was devoted to the town of Prague by prince Hanavský and in 1898 relocated from the area of the Exhibition grounds to the gardens in Letná where it has been ever since. Halfway to the Exhibition area, there is the Fair Palace which was built between 1925 and 1928 after a project by the architects Oldřich Tyl and Josef Fuchs. Today, it houses some of the collections of the National Gallery.

From Holešovice it is only a stone's throw away to Trója, a part of Prague which takes pride in the beautiful castle of the counts of Sternberg. The summer residence Trója was built in 1679–85 after a project by the architect Jean Baptista Mathey as country mansion of Roman architecture. A piece of architecture of distinctive beauty are the stairs with two flights leading to the garden with its statues made by the guild of Jan Jiří and Pavel Hermann (1685–1703) showing the fight of the Gods vs. the titans.

The Hill of Žižkov went down in history in 1420 as the place where the Hussite leader Jan Žižka of Trocnov defeated the crusade troops of Sigmund. In memory of this event, the monument, the work of the architect Jan Zázvorka, rose there between 1929 and 1932. In front of the monument, there is a gigantic bronze statue of the commander Žižka on a horse, the work of the sculptor Bohumil Kafka, a student of Myslbek.

Further and further agglomerations that arose in the 20th century were affiliated to Prague. They are mostly surrounded by the green belts opening out the town of Prague to all cardinal points. Today, the beauty of Prague is admired by visitors from all over the world: the vision of the princess Libuše has come true – Prague has become a town of worldwide fame and glory.

Golden Angel (Smíchov) – built according to the project of the architect Jean Nouvel

Bertramka – Monument of Mozart, Smíchov

Stadium of Sazka-Arena – Vysočany

Industrial Palace in the Fair Grounds Holešovice

Church of the Holy Heart of Our Lord – Vinohrady

The National Monument in Žižkov

Jewish Cemetery, Fibich Street – Žižkov

The tomb of Franz Kafka at the Jewish Cemetery in Žižkov

Hilton Hotel on the Rohan Embankment

The Renaissance summer residence 'Star' on the White Mountain

The Trade Fairs Palace, part of the National Gallery

Corinthia Hotel and Congress Palace – Pankrác

The small Hall of the Trade Fairs Palace. National Gallery

Troja Chateau

The baroque monastery church of St. Margaret in Břevnov